Will you be my Facebook friend?

SOCIAL MEDIA AND THE GOSPEL

10 Publishing
a division of 10ofthose.com

Will you be my Facebook friend?
© 10Publishing 2013 Tim Chester

Published in 2013 by 10Publishing, a division of 10ofthose.com

9D Centurion Court, Farington, Leyland, PR25 3UQ, England.

Email: info@10ofthose.com
Website: www.10ofthose.com

ISBN 9781906173852

Design by Diane Bainbridge
Printed by CPI Group (UK) Ltd, Croydon, CR0 4YY, England.

💬 Get off-line, turn off Spotify and read this book! You'll get through it in less time than many of us spend on Facebook each day, but this book will do you lasting good. Tim Chester writes honestly and urgently about both the potential and pitfalls of social media, calling us back to the 3D relationships we were created for. Like.
Dave Gobbett, Associate Pastor, Eden Baptist.

💬 It's striking, given the amount of time that many of us spend communicating with others online, how few of us have stopped to reflect on why we do so? This great little book will help you do just that, exposing wrong motives and showing us how faith in Christ challenges and changes the way we engage with others online.
Tim Dennis, UCCF Midlands Team Leader.

💬 Tim Chester is always insightful, and this little book is no exception. Wise, gracious, challenging and thoughtful, it will benefit anyone who uses social media. First class.
Andrew Wilson, Pastor, King's Church, Eastbourne.

💬 Do you check Facebook lots of times every day and wait expectantly for the little red notification signs? If so, this book is for you. It encourages us to think about how we can use Facebook (and other social media) in a way that keeps God at the centre of our lives, and glorify him not ourselves. A challenging and helpful read.

Sarah Bradley, Youth Minister and Keswick Youth Leader.

💬 This book is concise, insightful, challenging and compelling. If social media is something that you, or those around you, are engaged with, you'd do well to un-plug for a while and plug-in to what Tim has to say on the matter. Uncomfortable truths are presented alongside wise, gracious advice. Above all we are repeatedly pointed to Jesus and encouraged to live real lives, rooted in genuine community and marked by the gospel. Like.

Dai Hankey, Church Planter and Author.

Contents

+1 What's the Problem?

When Facebook launched on the NASDAQ stock exchange in May 2012, it was valued at over 100 billion dollars. Not bad for a company that had only been in existence for eight years. The website's revenue in 2011 was 3.7 billion dollars, up from 153 million in 2007. It is clearly offering its users something significant.

In just a few years, Facebook has gone from nothing to a major feature of modern life with over 500 million users, half of whom use it on any given day. More than 200 million users access Facebook through mobile devices. Facebook is itself part of the wider phenomenon of mobile technology and social networking or Web 2.0 – the use of the Internet not just to find information, but to connect with people. Social networking has rapidly become a significant aspect of the lives of many people today.

💬 Every minute of every day:[1]

- YouTube users upload forty-eight hours of new video
- email users send over 200 million messages
- Google receives over 2 million search queries
- Facebook users share over 680,000 pieces of content
- consumers spend £175,000 in online retailing
- Twitter users send over 100,000 tweets
- Tumblr users publish over 27,700 new posts
- Apple receives about 47,000 app downloads
- brands and organizations on Facebook receive almost 35,000 'likes'
- users of Flickr add 3,125 new photos
- Wordpress blog users (like me) publish 347 new posts
- 571 new websites are created
- the mobile web receives 217 new users

Every minute.

And I know this because I found the information online.

Benefits

There is much that is good about this. New technologies reflect humanity's God-given, Godlike creativity. God gave us a mandate to take his world and invent, create, produce.

Social networking brings many benefits.

One of my colleagues is from Australia. Looking over his shoulder in the office last week, I saw a video of his 2-year-old son. His wife had taken it moments before on her iPhone and then emailed it to the grandparents, copying in my colleague. New technologies are enabling people to keep in touch over long distances.

In the early days of email, our church was involved in sending missionaries to Azerbaijan. I remember a prayer meeting in which we prayed for the wife because she was struggling with a headache. We were all awed by the fact that we were praying for their prayer needs in much the same way as we were praying for the needs of one another. Instead of having to wait weeks at a time for letters that summarized months of news, we were able to pray for them in real time. Now texts, emails, blogs, Twitter and Skype enable missionaries to keep in constant touch with sending churches. These things may not replace face-to-face contact, but they are a big improvement on occasional letters.

New technologies are also enabling the message of Jesus to go into countries where missionaries cannot readily go, or to reinforce the work of missionaries on the ground. Once it was radio. Now websites and online TV channels bring the gospel to people while Skype and emails allow follow-up discipleship. I have Christian friends who are working with immigrants in the United Kingdom. They are able to give them readings of the Scriptures in their native language by sending audio files by Bluetooth between their phones.

People are able readily to organize events or arrange meetings. The recent change of regime in Egypt was called by some 'the Facebook revolution' because of the way Facebook was used to organize the protests. It is creating a culture of collaboration where products, campaigns, software and social enterprise can all be developed through cooperation.

We can all list the benefits in our own daily lives – from texting ahead to let someone know we are running late, to checking football scores when we are out, to reading the Bible on the commute home, to hearing about good resources through a blog or receiving an encouraging Tweet.

Dangers

But, despite all of this, there are also dangers. What's more, while the benefits of new technologies are immediately apparent, the negatives are more hidden. Tim Challies says: 'a technology wears its benefits on its sleeve – but the drawbacks are buried deep within.'[2] Technology is good. But it readily gets perverted by our sin, and used for selfish ends.

More than that, 'the medium is the message'. This is what the cultural critic Marshall McLuhan has alerted us to. In other words, *how* we communicate changes *what* we communicate.

The technology we use to express our thoughts actually changes those thoughts. It changes what we think is important.

Some problems with social networking are obvious.

Perhaps the clearest danger is the amount of time many of us spend using social media. Over 700 billion minutes are spent each month on Facebook. That is a lot of minutes.

Not only that, but more than half its users log on at least once every day. Nearly half of Facebook's users between the ages of 18 and 34 check Facebook within minutes of first waking up in the morning. Over a quarter of them do so before they even get out of bed.

The problem is not just quantity of time, but the constant interruption. Lots of people talk about Facebook as the greatest distraction from work ever. Students are suffering from lack of sleep because they are texting or on Facebook late into the night.

Remember, the medium is the message. In the

case of Twitter, this means thoughts must be expressed in 140 characters. For blogs it means around 400 words (anything more and people will not read it). Facebook, too, is designed to deliver short updates and comments. Not using proper grammar and sentences is affecting the way we express ideas. We are losing our ability to construct an argument. 'Internet users skim text rather than read it. In fact, "skimming" is now the dominant metaphor for reading.'[3]

The combination of Google and smart phones mean we access information whenever we like and this is changing our attitude to ideas. Why learn historical dates when you can look them up on Wikipedia? The problem is that no longer holding information in our minds prevents us making connections between ideas. Or, if forgetting a few historical dates seems harmless, let me rephrase the question: Why learn Bible verses when you can look them up on your iPhone? Yet the Bible itself invites us to meditate on and retain its words. 'I have hidden your word in my heart', says the psalmist, 'that I might not sin against you' (Ps. 119:11). Jesus said: 'If you remain in me and my words remain in you, ask whatever you wish, and it will be given you' (John 15:7). Chuck Swindoll wrote:

> 💬 *I know of no other single practice in the Christian life more rewarding, practically speaking, than memorizing Scripture... No other single exercise pays greater spiritual dividends! Your prayer life will be strengthened. Your witnessing will be sharper and much more effective. Your attitudes and outlook will begin to change. Your mind will become alert and observant. Your confidence and assurance will be enhanced. Your faith will be solidified.[4]*

What is it that drives this concern for brevity and this constant movement to new content? The answer is commercial interests. What is Facebook's product? It is you. You are its product, delivered in large quantities to advertisers! It is the same with Google. They make money when you click on adverts, so it is in their interest for you never to spend long on one page. The medium is designed to keep you constantly surfing, constantly skimming, constantly clicking. And this is reducing our ability to concentrate. We zip from one piece of information to another. We keep stopping to check texts, emails, tweets, Facebook. People increasingly find it hard to concentrate for an extended period on a complex argument.

Technology makes us more efficient. And efficiency is good. But only in some contexts. Do you want to be an efficient lover? An efficient parent? An efficient worshipper?

But all these things are just the symptoms. The real issue is this: Why do people spend so much time on Facebook? Why do they feel the need to check and recheck their social media? What does it *do* for them? What does it offer?

Problems?

These questions matter because it is not enough simply to say 'Stop' or 'Do it less'. If the only response you can give me is to be more self-controlled then you are inviting me to be my own saviour. Suppose you stop reading at this point, and leave this booklet determined to use Facebook less. You may succeed, in which case you will probably feel pretty proud of yourself. Or you may struggle to wean yourself off your social media, in which case you will probably feel pretty bad about yourself. You are reliant on willpower. It is the way of legalism. The Bible says rules on their own have no power to make us godly (Col. 2:20–23). Even on a good day legalism leads to pride, because the focus is on *our* efforts.

We need instead to see how Christ offers more. It is the grace of God that leads to self-control. 'For the grace of God that brings salvation has appeared to all men. It teaches us to say "No" to ungodliness and worldly passions, and to live self-controlled, upright and godly lives in this present age' (Titus 2:11,12). In this case, Christ more than meets the needs that social media appear to satisfy for us. When we grasp the goodness of Christ then the focus of change is not on us, but on him, and any change brings him glory rather than us.

In the case of social media we also need to look

at why some people find using it so compulsive, because some of us may not be convinced we need saving from it! Why give up something I think is good? And social media *are* good. As we have seen, they bring many benefits. The problem is that their dominance in some of our lives may be a sign that we are turning to them when we should be turning to God. We are not going to give up something we find good until we recognize that something better is on offer.

So the key question is: Why? This enables us to make the gospel the answer.

For countless people, of course, using Facebook is not a problem. For many it is all blessing. But there are dangers in social networking, and here are some possible warning signs:

- Do you check your Facebook page more than once or twice a day?
- Do you spend more than twenty minutes a day on Facebook?
- Do you find it difficult to imagine a day without technology?

- Have you ever read a text or gone online during a church gathering?

- Have you stayed up beyond your normal bedtime because you were on Facebook or playing online games?

- Do you use your mobile phone during meals or keep it in the bedroom?

Those are some warning signs. What are the dangers? What is it about Facebook that makes it so addictive?

---

1 Source:www.visualnews.com/2012/06/19/how-much-data-created-every-minute.

2 Tim Challies, *The Next Story: Life and Faith After the Digital Explosion* (Grand Rapids, MI: Zondervan, 2011).

3 Tim Challies, *The Next Story: Life and Faith After the Digital Explosion* (Grand Rapids, MI: Zondervan, 2011).

4 Charles R. Swindoll, *Growing Strong in the Seasons of Life* (Grand Rapids, MI: Zondervan, 1994) p.61.

+2 Recreating My World

The first reason many of us find Facebook so compulsive is that *on Facebook I can recreate my world through my words to gain approval.*

Think about the name 'Facebook'. It suggests a place where I can show my 'face' or my 'image'.

---

1. I Can Recreate My 'Face'

One reason Facebook is popular is because it appears to allow me to create my image using my words. I type in a version of the person I want to be. I use my words to create a positive image. Or I upload pictures that portray me in a certain way, usually having a good time or looking beautiful in artistic poses. There are no pictures of me first thing in the morning or being bored.

Celebrity culture pours over the minutiae of the lives of the rich and famous. Facebook, blogs and Twitter allow us all to be celebrities with our lives on show. It blurs the public and the private. The world becomes my audience. On Facebook you do not have a conversation, you have an audience. Your life takes place on a stage and you are your own playwright, creating or recreating yourself through your words.

2. I Can Recreate My 'Space'

This is the genius of Facebook, MySpace and other social networking sites. Facebook enables me to have all my friends and family gathered in one place. What we cannot do in physical space, we can do in cyberspace: bring everyone together in one place. But this is *my* space. The name 'MySpace' is a clue – it suggests a space over which I have dominion. This is my world.

The genius of Facebook is that all your friends come to you and all their friends come to them. So we simultaneously all inhabit our own little worlds, each with me at the centre.

These people are by definition my 'chosen people'. In the Bible the 'chosen people' are God's people, graciously chosen by him. When we come to faith we find ourselves part of a concrete expression of God's chosen people in our local church. God fits us together so we can grow together towards maturity in Christ (Eph. 4:11–16). God has chosen the people in your church so they can help you come to maturity and so you can help them come to maturity. But social media allows us to play God and create our own chosen people. And we are at the centre of this chosen circle.

One pastor told me: 'The people I know who use Facebook most are those who are most self-obsessed.' I remember a young woman who wrote a blog about her life. But like most of us, her life was pretty boring. So she constantly had to heighten the sense of drama. Her blog became the story of her heroic struggle to overcome really quite minor difficulties. The result was she thought of life as a constant self-obsessed melodrama. An Australian study entitled 'Who Uses Facebook?' found a significant correlation between the use of Facebook and narcissism. 'Facebook users have higher levels of total narcissism, exhibitionism, and leadership than Facebook nonusers', the study reported. 'In fact, it could be argued that

Facebook specifically gratifies the narcissistic individual's need to engage in self-promoting and superficial behaviour.'[5]

3. I Can Find Approval

Not only do I create or recreate myself through my words on Facebook, but I can *measure* myself through Facebook. I can rank my image through the number of my Facebook friends or Twitter followers. I can score myself through the number of 'Likes' on my Facebook wall or the number of 'comments' my blog post receives. These become the index of my self-worth. Or I do visual assessments by comparing photos. Jonny Woodrow, associate director of the Porterbrook Seminary, calls it 'personality by numbers'.

Notice, too, from whom I am seeking approval. I am defined by other people's 'gaze', what they make of my 'face'. The Bible calls this 'the fear of man'. Our overriding concern should be what God thinks of me. But instead my concern is what other users of social media think of me. It is their approval that matters. In contrast, Paul says: 'Am I now trying to win the approval of men, or of God? Or am I trying to please men? If I were still trying to please men, I would not be a servant of Christ' (Gal. 1:10). 'I care very little if I am judged by you or by any human court; indeed, I do not even judge myself. My conscience is clear, but that does not make me innocent. It is the Lord who judges me' (1 Cor. 4:3,4). It is hard to imagine the man who wrote these words worrying too much whether his Facebook comments had received 'Likes' or how many Twitter followers he had! What mattered to him was the approval of God.

On Facebook I receive approval and I bestow approval. The result is that many people constantly check their Facebook page because this is where they receive affirmation.

Notice the language we are using. I recreate my image through my words. I recreate my world around me. I can find approval or justify myself. This is the salvation language. This is gospel language. Facebook – used in this way – is another gospel. *I am recreating my image and my world through my words so that I find approval or justify myself.*

Does this work? Does self-creation or self-justification through Facebook work?

Alex Jordan of Stanford University found people often feel depressed after spending time on Facebook.[6] To understand why, you have got to remember that the medium is the message. How we communicate shapes what we communicate. And Facebook is geared to project positivity. You upload pictures of people having a good time, not pictures of you feeling bored or miserable. Even the jokey, early morning shots of people looking rough are really saying, 'Look, me *after* I've had a good time.' Compared to all these photos, the day I have just had at work seems dull or sad.

People can 'Like' something you have written. But there is no option to 'Dislike'. So to get a response you have to phrase things in positive terms. No one is going to click 'Like' to 'Had a miserable day at work'. So instead you put, 'Looking forward to watching a movie with a tub of ice cream.' 'Like'! No one is going to click 'Like' to 'My rabbit died yesterday.' So instead you put, 'Fluffy was a brave little bunny until the very end.' 'Like'!

So everyone's Facebook face wears a smile – whatever the reality behind the mask. We are all spin doctors, presenting upbeat propaganda versions of our lives.

So the typical process the research revealed goes something like this: You are feeling miserable. You go onto Facebook. Everyone you know appears happy. So you feel a loser. All the time you forget that somewhere someone else is looking at your upbeat, unreal Facebook page and feeling like *they* are missing out.

There are exceptions. There are people who like to bemoan how difficult their life is. They too 'spin' their lives, but their message is misery. What they have in common with people who portray an upbeat version of their life is self-obsession. There is a significant online community for people with disorders such as anorexia providing mutual encouragement and even competing at suffering. Again, the desire to portray yourself as a success is the same, it is just that the criteria of success are different – in this case how thin you are or how miserable you are.

Here is the test of whether you are facing this danger: *Is your Facebook self more attractive or successful than your real-world self?*

The real question is: Am I trying to do self-identity or am I finding identity in Christ? Or: Am I looking for approval from others through my words, or approval from God through his gospel word?

This project of self-justification is doomed to fail because we cannot justify ourselves. The problem is that for some people this failure simply spurs them on to post and repost, check and recheck.

💬 Not only must we contend with the social bounty of others; we must foster the appearance of our own social bounty. Being happy all the time, pretending to be happy, actually attempting to be happy – it's exhausting… The relentlessness is what is so new, so potentially transformative. Facebook never takes a break. We never take a break. Human beings have always created elaborate acts of self-presentation. But not all the time, not every morning, before we even pour a cup of coffee.[7]

If this analysis sounds far-fetched or over-spiritualized, then ask yourself this simple question: Suppose I told you to give up all your social media for a month. How would you respond? Easy? Or does that sound impossible? Are you making your excuses even as you read?

To those of us exhausted by the need to portray themselves for the approval of others, Jesus says: 'Come to me, all you who are weary and burdened, and I will give you rest' (Matt. 11:28).

The gospel of Jesus says that Jesus recreates me in the image of God, and Jesus is recreating the world. God's kingdom is extended as his word is proclaimed.

Jesus recreates me – I'm not a self-made person.

Jesus recreates me in God's image – it's not about my image.

Jesus recreates the world – I'm not the saviour.

Jesus recreates God's world – it's not my world.

Jesus creates God's world with God at the centre – not me at the centre.

Jesus creates and recreates through God's word – not through my words.

It is these truths that enable me to be truly human, fit for the purpose for which I was created. And this is what liberates me from self-obsession to enjoy the goodness and grace of God. Knowing the real God is better than Facebook.

....

[5] Cited in Stephen Marche, 'Is Facebook Making Us Lonely?', *The Atlantic*, May 2012, www.theatlantic.com/magazine/archive/2012/05/is-facebook-making-us-lonely/8930.

[6] Alex Jordan, 'Misery Has More Company Than People Think', *Personality and Social Psychology Bulletin*, cited in Libby Copeland, 'The Anti-Social Network', Slate, 26 January 2011, slate.com/id/2282620.

[7] Stephen Marche, 'Is Facebook Making Us Lonely?', *The Atlantic*, May 2012, www.theatlantic.com/magazine/archive/2012/05/is-facebook-making-us-lonely/8930.

+3 Escaping My Limitations

A second reason we can find Facebook addictive is that *on Facebook I can escape the limitations of my body*.

Our bodies limit us to a particular place and time. We can only be in one place at a time.

Facebook, however, promises to connect us with everyone everywhere at any time. It promises omniscience (knowing everything) and omnipresence (being everywhere). But in the real world, omniscience and omnipresence are attributes of God alone, so social media cannot deliver – not if you want real relationships and real community.

We have already said that the Internet encourages us to skim read everything. Facebook extends the same idea into personal relationships. We can now do skim befriending or surface friendships.

Facebook offers intimacy without responsibility. People say things on Facebook to people or about people that they would never say if they were physically in the room with them.

👍 29

People say things *about* people they would not say in the flesh. A church planter friend told me Facebook has caused havoc in his neighbourhood because of the way it spreads gossip. Seventeen per cent of employees in large companies have been reprimanded for words they have written on Facebook.

People say things *to* people they would not say in the flesh. In May 2012, Mark Zuckerberg, the founder of Facebook, changed his status to 'married' and received over one million 'Likes'. But Facebook is not always so marriage-friendly. A recent newspaper article highlighted one lawyer who has dealt with thirty divorce cases in the last year, and Facebook has been implicated in them all.[8] Online flirting is leading to real-world relational breakdown. More than a third of UK divorce filings in 2011 contained the word 'Facebook'. Over 80 per cent of US divorce lawyers say they have seen a rise in divorces involving social networking. K. Jason Krafsky, author of *Facebook and Your Marriage*, says, 'Affairs happen with a lightning speed on Facebook.' Office romances took time to develop, and that meant time to think about what you were doing. Facebook connects us both with old flames and passing contacts whom we might otherwise forget. 'It puts temptation in the path of people who would never in a million years risk having an affair.'[9]

Proverbs 10:19 says: 'When words are many, sin is not absent, but he who holds his tongue is wise.' Facebook does not cause sin, but it can accelerate it because it liberates it from the constraints of the body.

An Embodied Life

Facebook offers us the ability to redefine ourselves and construct our own world without being constrained by others. But our bodies remind us that this is not our world. We literally bump into people. We collide. You cannot look round a crowded room and say, 'This is my world and I'm at the centre.' Our bodies remind us that we live in a world created by the words of someone else – by the words of God. And we live in a world created *for* someone else – for the glory of God.

It is the same with porn and online role-playing games. They offer liberation from the body. You compensate for your real-world inadequacies, fears, struggles, with a fantasy world in which you are potent and successful with endless beautiful people offering themselves to you.

Cyberspace offers an escape from the limitations of the body. And this version of 'salvation by Facebook' is the latest embodiment (pun intended) of the ancient heresy of Gnosticism. Gnosticism saw the spiritual or mental as good and the body as evil and limiting. So salvation was an escape from the constraints of the body.

Tim Challies talks about 'digital disincarnation'.[10] 'Incarnation' is the word we use to describe the event of God becoming man, of God taking on human flesh. But now in cyberspace we are trying to 'disincarnate', to throw off the limitations of human flesh. Challies says: 'Here in the cyberworld I can be popular. I can be powerful. I can be somebody. And yet I do it all at the expense of who I really am.'[11]

In contrast, the gospel affirms the body. The gospel says that human beings were made by God with a body, and God declared that to be good. We were made with bodies in his image to reflect his image in the world. More than that, God himself takes on human flesh when Jesus becomes a man. Christ 'appeared in a body [and] was vindicated by the Spirit' (1 Tim. 3:16). And, more than that, the body of Jesus was *physically* raised from the dead. The resurrection of Jesus was not an escape from the body, but the redemption of the body. So the gospel encourages us to engage in embodied life and embodied relationships.

So Paul says to the Christian community in Thessalonica: 'We loved you so much that we were delighted to share with you not only the gospel of God but our lives as well, because you had become so dear to us' (1 Thess. 2:8). 'But since we were torn away from you, brothers, for a short time, in person not in heart, we endeavoured the more eagerly and with great desire to see you face to face' (1 Thess. 2:17, ESV). Not just words, but a shared life. Not just words, but face to face. Not just an online 'face', but face to face. Not just an online presence, but an embodied presence.

Professor Barry Wellman of Toronto University talks of 'networked individualism'.[12] We can move from one online community to another. We can drop, forget, invite or ignore Facebook 'friends' at will without consequences. We build our own worlds.

God has placed you together with the people in your congregation. You did not choose them; God chose them. And that diversity of personalities, backgrounds, social class and ethnicities is used by God to make you grow in Christ and to display the unifying power of the cross.

But in cyberspace *you* are God. *You* choose who will be in community with you. You create your own communities of convenience that mean you are never challenged. Or, if you are challenged or relationships become costly, you can just scuttle off to new relationships. As a result we never grow. We are permanently immature.

In cyberspace no relationship is meaningful and every relationship is expendable. The result is loneliness in the midst of many Facebook 'friends'. A recent Australian study found that lonely people spend more time on Facebook: 'One of the most noteworthy findings', they wrote, 'was the tendency for neurotic and lonely individuals to spend greater amounts of time on Facebook per day than non-lonely individuals.'[13]

I know people for whom Facebook is a place to hide. You can think of yourself surrounded by friends without ever having to engage with the challenges of real-world relationships. You have a lot of friends, a 'loose electronic Diaspora',[14] without ever really being known. Your idolatries, your selfishness, your struggles are never seen. Instead a lot of people get the sanitized version of you. Moreover most of us praise in public and rebuke in private. So, because Facebook is a public medium, people are generally going to make positive comments. Challenges to our behaviour are left unsaid. Facebook is a safe place to hide from real relationships.

Many people struggle to do everything they want to do. But I can give you an extra hour each day! I have the secret. Think what you could do with an extra hour: time with the children, doing mission, reading your Bible, learning a new skill. What is the answer? Stop using Facebook. On average, users spend twenty hours a month on Facebook. That is the average, which means getting on for 250 million people are spending up to an hour or more on it. You could stop. Some people do not have a Facebook page and somehow life goes on. And you get another hour each day.

Some of us have little time for community life and missional endeavour because we are spending too much time on Facebook or watching television or surfing blogs. We are opting for disembodied life over embodied life.

In many ways, disembodied life is easier. But it is less fulfilling, less real and less satisfying. Embodied life is harder. But it is more fulfilling, more real, more satisfying. It is more substantial – you can touch it, feel it, embrace it!

Men, for example, should be taking responsibility in their homes, workplaces, churches or neighbourhoods. But many young men today are spending hours on their Xbox and never really growing up. There is nothing intrinsically wrong with computer games. But many of us are playing with toys when we could be taking risks for Christ's kingdom or leading the way in new gospel initiatives. Our culture encourages men not to grow up. It says: 'Think of yourself as ten years younger than you are and you will be happy.'

So men are spending evenings playing Halo when they could be serving in their church youth group or moving into a needy area to share Christ. They are opting for the pseudo-machismo of the virtual warrior rather than risk becoming warriors in the real spiritual battle. They are remaining boys rather than becoming men.

One study found that over half of young women spend more time talking to people online than face to face. Another study found that for every hour we spend on our computers, face-to-face interaction falls by thirty minutes. The more people engage online, the less able they are to engage offline. Real-world communication feels more threatening, less natural, less normal.

I was talking to the wife of a church leader. She was describing how many people struggle to keep up with old friends. They are often pulled away from church and mission to visit people elsewhere in the country. And Facebook perpetuates this. The result is thin relationships. In contrast, she talked about how as a couple they recognized that God has placed them in their city, in a physical place with physical bodies with all the limitations that involves. So they have chosen to focus on the people in their Christian community and their neighbourhood. They do not give a lot of time to 'keeping up' with past relationships. They focus on their present time and their present place. As a result they have relationships that are deep and significant.

The apostle John knew the value of written communication. He wrote one of the Gospels, three New Testament letters and the book of Revelation. And yet it is clear that he preferred face-to-face communication. 'Though I have much to write to you, I would rather not use paper and ink. Instead I hope to come to you and talk *face to face*, so that our joy may be complete' (2 John 12, ESV, italics mine); 'I have much to write to you, but I do not want to do so with pen and ink. I hope to see you soon, and we will talk *face to face*' (3 John 13,14, italics mine). We need to ensure we have the same preference for face-to-face communication over Facebook-to-Facebook communication. It is often said that in the struggle with sin and the struggle to make Christ known we need people who will stand with us, fight with us and die for us. I suspect we will not find such people among our Facebook friends, unless they are also face-to-face friends.

Facebook encourages you to live elsewhere. The gospel encourages you to live life here and now.

- You can tend your FarmVille farm or you can get an allotment.
- You can catch up with friends on Facebook or you can go out on a cold, dark night to see real friends.
- You can catch up with *Friends* by watching the latest episode on the television or you can serve your neighbours.
- You can build a new city on Sims or you can be the city of God set on a hill with your Christian community.

Here is the test: *Am I using Facebook to enhance real-world friendships, or to replace them?*

John Cacioppo from the University of Chicago looked at the correlation between loneliness of his study's subjects and their use of Facebook and other social media. 'The greater the proportion of face-to-face interactions, the less lonely you are...' he says. 'The greater the proportion of online interactions, the lonelier you are.' But, he concluded, it is not that Facebook inevitably makes you lonelier. 'If you use Facebook to increase face-to-face contact', he says, 'it increases social capital.'[15] In other words, if you use social media to arrange to meet up with friends at a coffee shop or organize a game of football, then social media will enhance your friendships. But if you use it as an alternative to face-to-face, contact then it will increase your loneliness.

---

8 Richard Alleyne, 'Facebook Increasingly Implicated in Divorce', *The Daily Telegraph*, 21 January 2011, www.telegraph.co.uk/technology/facebook/8274601/Facebook-increasingly-implicated-in-divorce.html.

9 K. Jason Krafsky, cited in Quentin Fottrell, 'Does Facebook Wreck Marriages?', SmartMoney.com, 21 May 2012, blogs.smartmoney.com/advice/2012/05/21/does-facebook-wreck-marriages.

10 Tim Challies, *The Next Story: Life and Faith After the Digital Explosion* (Grand Rapids, MI: Zondervan, 2011).

11 ibid.

12 ibid.

13 Cited in Stephen Marche, 'Is Facebook Making Us Lonely?', *The Atlantic*, May 2012, www.theatlantic.com/magazine/archive/2012/05/is-facebook-making-us-lonely/8930.

14 James Harkin, 'Living in Cyburbia', *The Daily Telegraph*, 29 January 2011, www.telegraph.co.uk/technology/social-media/8289324/Living-in-Cyburbia.html

15 Cited in Stephen Marche, 'Is Facebook Making Us Lonely?', *The Atlantic*, May 2012, www.theatlantic.com/magazine/archive/2012/05/is-facebook-making-us-lonely/8930.

+4 The Face Book of God

As we conclude, I want to reiterate that for many people, using Facebook is not a problem. For many it is all blessing.

But there are dangers in social networking. And to those who face those dangers, the gospel provides a better and richer alternative.

Facebook is the place where I show my face or my image. For some of you it is the place were you recreate your image and your world through your words. **The gospel** is the place where God turns 'his face towards us' (see Num. 6:26). It is the place where he recreates us in his image and recreates his world through his words.

2 Corinthians 3:18 says: 'And we, who with unveiled faces all reflect the Lord's glory, are being transformed into his likeness with ever-increasing glory, which comes from the Lord, who is the Spirit.'

Through Facebook you can show your face or image to the world. **Through the gospel** we see the face of God, the glory of God. And when we see it, we radiate that glory just as Moses did long ago when he saw God on Mount Sinai. Through the gospel we can reflect the glory of God to the world.

Through Facebook we can recreate ourselves. We can recreate our own identity to win the approval of other people. **Through the gospel** *God* recreates us in the image of *Jesus*. Jesus makes us approved by God. And we are being transformed into the likeness of Jesus with ever-increasing glory. Look at your Facebook page: Do you really want this more than the glory of God?

Remember the medium is the message, and Facebook was designed by a teenage nerd. It reduces your life to the preoccupations of a student nerd. You are encouraged to fill in your relationship status because students define themselves by their 'availability'. The medium encourages you to express your personality through lists of books, movies, TV programmes. This is what nerdy students do. You are encouraged to poke people – poking is what teenage boys do who do not know how to talk to girls. The medium is the message. Your life is being squeezed down into these select, nerdy categories. You can give your time to this – or to being transformed into Christ's likeness with ever-increasing glory.

2 Corinthians 4:5: 'For we do not preach ourselves, but Jesus Christ as Lord, and ourselves as your servants for Jesus' sake.'

Through Facebook we can promote ourselves. We gain friends. Or we gain followers through Twitter. We engage in self-evangelism. **Through the gospel** we promote Jesus as Lord. We gain followers for Jesus.

2 Corinthians 4:6: 'For God, who said, "Let light shine out of darkness," made his light shine in our hearts to give us the light of the knowledge of the glory of God in the face of Christ.'

Through Facebook we recreate our world through our words. Day after day, endless words pour out as we try to create an image of ourselves that others will approve. And **God speaks** four words, 'Let there be light.' Two words in Hebrew.

And there is light. God speaks and the universe comes into being. This physical, substantial, real universe. The kind of universe you can hit with your hand and it hurts because it is really there.

Through Facebook we reveal our 'face' and look at the 'faces' of other people. **Through the gospel** we see the face of God. The Bible is the true Facebook, the book in which we see God's face. Prayer is the ultimate instant messaging. The church is the real social network. The gospel is the place where we see 'the light of the knowledge of the glory of God in the face of Christ.' Columnist Stephen Marche says:

> Solitude used to be good for self-reflection and self-reinvention. But now we are left thinking about who we are all the time, without ever *really* thinking about who we are. Facebook denies us a pleasure whose profundity we had underestimated: the chance to forget about ourselves for a while, the chance to disconnect.[16] *(my italics)*

Or, better still, the chance to reconnect with the triune God.

Seeking God's Face

Think about what you have written and read on your Facebook wall this week. Think about the tweets you have followed. Imagine reading them in six months' time. I suspect that much of what is written will be drivel. Trivia. Empty. 'Eating egg on toast. Yum.' 'On my way to the station.' 'Great party last night.' 'Jack just fell over. LOL.' 'Love the photos – you're so gorgeous.' Poke. Listen to the prophet Isaiah:

> *A voice says, 'Cry out.'*
> *And I said, 'What shall I cry?'*
> *'All men are like grass,*
> *and all their glory is like the flowers of the field.*
> *The grass withers and the flowers fall,*
> *because the breath of the LORD blows on them.*
> *Surely the people are grass.*
> *The grass withers and the flowers fall,*
> *but the word of our God stands forever.'*
>
> **(Isa. 40:6–8)**

Or to paraphrase:

> *The Facebook comments wither*
> *and the tweets fall,*
> *but the word of our God stands forever.*

What will you give your time to this week? Trivia? Or the word of our God that stands forever?

The psalmist says: 'My heart says of you, "Seek his face!" Your face, LORD, I will seek' (Ps. 27:8).

---

[16] Stephen Marche, 'Is Facebook Making Us Lonely?', *The Atlantic*, May 2012, www.theatlantic.com/magazine/archive/2012/05/is-facebook-making-us-lonely/8930.

+ Twelve Guidelines for Social Networking

I want to conclude with some guidelines. I do not want to be too prescriptive about these. But they may be useful to someone who feels themselves susceptible to the dangers we have highlighted.

1. Don't say anything online that you wouldn't say were the people concerned in the room.

2. Don't say anything online that you wouldn't share publicly with your Christian community.

3. Ensure your online world is visible to your offline Christian community.

4. Challenge one another if you think someone's online self reflects a self-created identity rather than identity in Christ.

5. Challenge one another if you think someone's online self doesn't match their offline self.

6. Use social networking to enhance real-world relationships, not to replace them.

7. Don't let children have unsupervised Internet access or accept as online friends people you don't know offline.

8. Set limits to the time you spend online and ask someone to hold you accountable to these.

9. Set aside a day a week as a technology 'Sabbath' or 'fast'.

10. Avoid alerts (emails, tweets, texts and so on) that interrupt other activities, especially reading, praying, worshipping and relating.

11. Ban mobiles from the meal table and the bedroom.

12. Look for opportunities to replace disembodied (online or phone) communication with embodied (face-to-face) communication.